CW00429112

Funny Tips & A...............
to Stay Calm
for Mums of Teenagers

This book belongs to

 – Tip

 – Affirmation

Don your
favourite superhero costume
when you need an extra
boost of confidence to
navigate your teenager's
mood swings.

Affirmation

I am
the problem-solving
superhero and no
teenager tantrum can
defeat me.

Wear noise-cancelling headphones when your teenager is blaring music or arguing with you.
It will be like your own little zen retreat.

Affirmation

I am the queen of snacks and will always have a stash for my hungry teenager.

Be a ninja and use your stealth moves to avoid stepping on the minefield of your teenager's moods.

Affirmation

I have the power to
make my teenager
laugh, even when they
are not in a good
mood.

Treat your teenager's
sarcastic comments like a
stand-up comedy routine.
Laugh it off and show
them you've got a
good sense of humour.

Affirmation

I am the conqueror
of teenage drama,
and my calmness
will win.

Create a Yell jar for yourself,
and deposit money every time
you feel like yelling at your
teenager.
You'll either end up with a lot of
money to spend on something for
the household, or you'll be
a much calmer mum.

Affirmation

I am the fairy godmother of laundry, and my teenager's dirty clothes on her *floordrobe will disappear with a wave of my wand.

*floordrobe = clothes all over the floor instead of in the wardrobe

Use emojis
to communicate with
your teen.
It's a lighthearted and fun way
to have a conversation.

Affirmation

I am the protector of curfews, and my teenager shall obey.

Pretend you're a referee
and use a whistle to
break up arguments between
your teenager and
their siblings.

Affirmation

My teenager's mood swings are no match for my patience and understanding

Use a megaphone to get your teenager's attention. It's an unexpected and fun way to communicate with them.

Affirmation

I am the ninja of negotiation, and my teenager will learn to compromise.

Use a silly voice when you're talking to your teenager. It will help to lighten the mood and just might make them laugh.

Affirmation

I am the queen of hugs and my teenager will always have a safe place to go.

Create a dance routine with
your teenager as a way
to bond and stay active. It's
also a fun way to release
stress and tension.

Affirmation

I am a detective of social media, and my teenager's online activity will not go unnoticed.

Practise your deep breathing techniques when your teenager is driving you crazy. It's a good way to stay calm and centered.

Affirmation

I am the self-care coach, and my teenager will see the importance of taking care of themselves.

Make a secret code word
or phrase with your teenager
that means "I need a break"
or "Let's change the subject".
It's a gentle way to
communicate without causing
a scene.

Affirmation

I am the captain of
our family ship, and
my teenager will learn
to navigate the waters
of life.

Use a toy lightsaber to block your teenager's negative energy. It's a fun way to show them that you don't take their grumpiness too seriously.

Affirmation

I am the queen of corny jokes and my teenager will learn to appreciate my humour.

Treat your teenager's mood swings like a rollercoaster ride. Strap in and enjoy the ride. It will eventually come to an end.

Affirmation

I am the ninja of patience, and my teenager will not break me.

Start a pillow fight with your teenager when you need to release some tension. It's a fun way to bond and let off steam.

Affirmation

I am the captain of
the kitchen, and my
teenager will learn to
appreciate my
cooking.

Wear a silly wig or hat when dealing with your teenager's moods. It's a great way to lighten the mood and show them that you're not bothered.

Affirmation

I am the queen of the
messy room, and my
teenager will
learn to tidy up
after themselves.

Put on a fake accent when you're feeling stressed. It's a fun way to pretend you're living in a completely different world.

Affirmation

I am the guru of forgiveness, and my teenager will learn from my example.

Wear a funny t-shirt that says
'World's Most Patient Mum'
or
'I am Surviving the Teenage Years'.
It's a great way to show your sense of humour and not take things too seriously.

Affirmation

I am the zen master of the family, and my teenager will learn to find inner peace.

Bring out your best dance moves when navigating your teenager's mood. It's a great way to lighten the atmosphere and show them you're not fussed.

Affirmation

I am the champion of our family game night, and my teenager will learn to have fun.

Play a game of charades with your teenager when you're having trouble communicating. It's a fun way to get everyone laughing.

Affirmation

I am the
family schedule
wizard and my
teenager will learn to
follow it.

Create a playlist of young children's songs to listen to and/or sing when you're feeling overwhelmed. It's a great way to boost your mood and not take things too seriously.

Affirmation

I am the captain of the homework battle, and my teenager will eventually see the light, and just get it done.

Put on some loud music
and dance like you have
no cares in the world.
It's a great way to release
some tension.

Affirmation

I am the defender
of family time, and
my teenager will not
interrupt our
quality time.

Use a squeaky toy to grab your teenager's attention when they're not listening. It's a fun way to communicate without raising your voice.

Affirmation

I am the superhero
of teenage emotions,
and my empathy will
save the day.

Wear a superhero cape when you're feeling overwhelmed. It's a great way to boost your confidence and show your teenager you're not easily defeated.

Affirmation

I am the magician of the family budget, and my teen will learn to appreciate the value of money.

Embrace your inner teenager and join in with your teenager's hobbies and interests. It's a great way to bond and stay connected.

Affirmation

I am the jester of the family, and my teenager will learn to lighten up

Treat yourself to a chocolate bar every time you successfully avoid an argument with your teenager. It's a delicious reward for staying calm.

Affirmation

I am the champion of the one-liner comeback, and my teenager will learn to fear my wittiness.

Put a positive spin on everything your teenager says, even if it's negative. It's a great way to stay optimistic and focus on the positive.

Affirmation

I am the guru
of screen time, and
my teenager will learn
to unplug.

Use a puppet to communicate with your teenager. It may be a silly but effective way to lighten the mood.

Affirmation

I am the keeper of
family traditions, and
my teenager will learn
to cherish them.

Use dice or a coin to make decisions when you're feeling indecisive. It takes the pressure off and makes for a fun game.

Affirmation

I am the manager of the thermostat, and my teenager will learn to dress appropriately.

Use a silly voice when talking to your teenager. It may lighten the mood and actually make them smile...or laugh at you.

Affirmation

I am the queen of embarrassment, and my teenager will learn to appreciate my dance moves.

Remember to laugh at yourself and not take things too seriously.

Parenting a teenager can be challenging, but it can also be hilarious and rewarding.

Affirmation

I am the steward of family happiness, and my teenager will learn to appreciate my efforts.

Write your own lighthearted tip for being
a mum of a teenager.

_____

_____

_____

_____

Write your own lighthearted affirmation
for being a mum of a teenager.

_____

_____

_____

_____

Write your own lighthearted tip for being a mum of a teenager.

_____

_____

_____

_____

Write your own lighthearted affirmation for being a mum of a teenager.

_____

_____

_____

_____

DECISION-MAKING DICE

Create your own dice by writing six decisions. Cut along the outside. Fold in the flaps. Secure with tape.

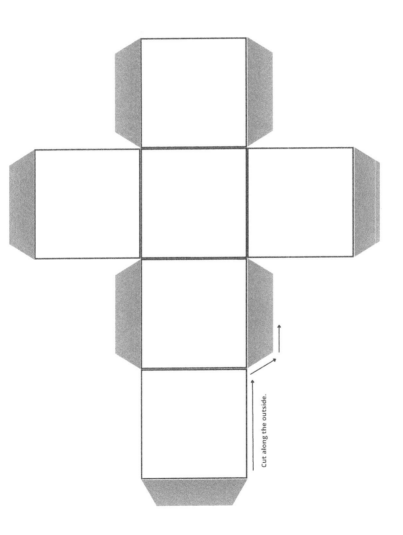

Cut along the outside.

Printed in Great Britain
by Amazon